Flowers From My Journey
A Collection of Poems
by

Dr. Kathryn D. Arnett, DSW, LCSW, CADC

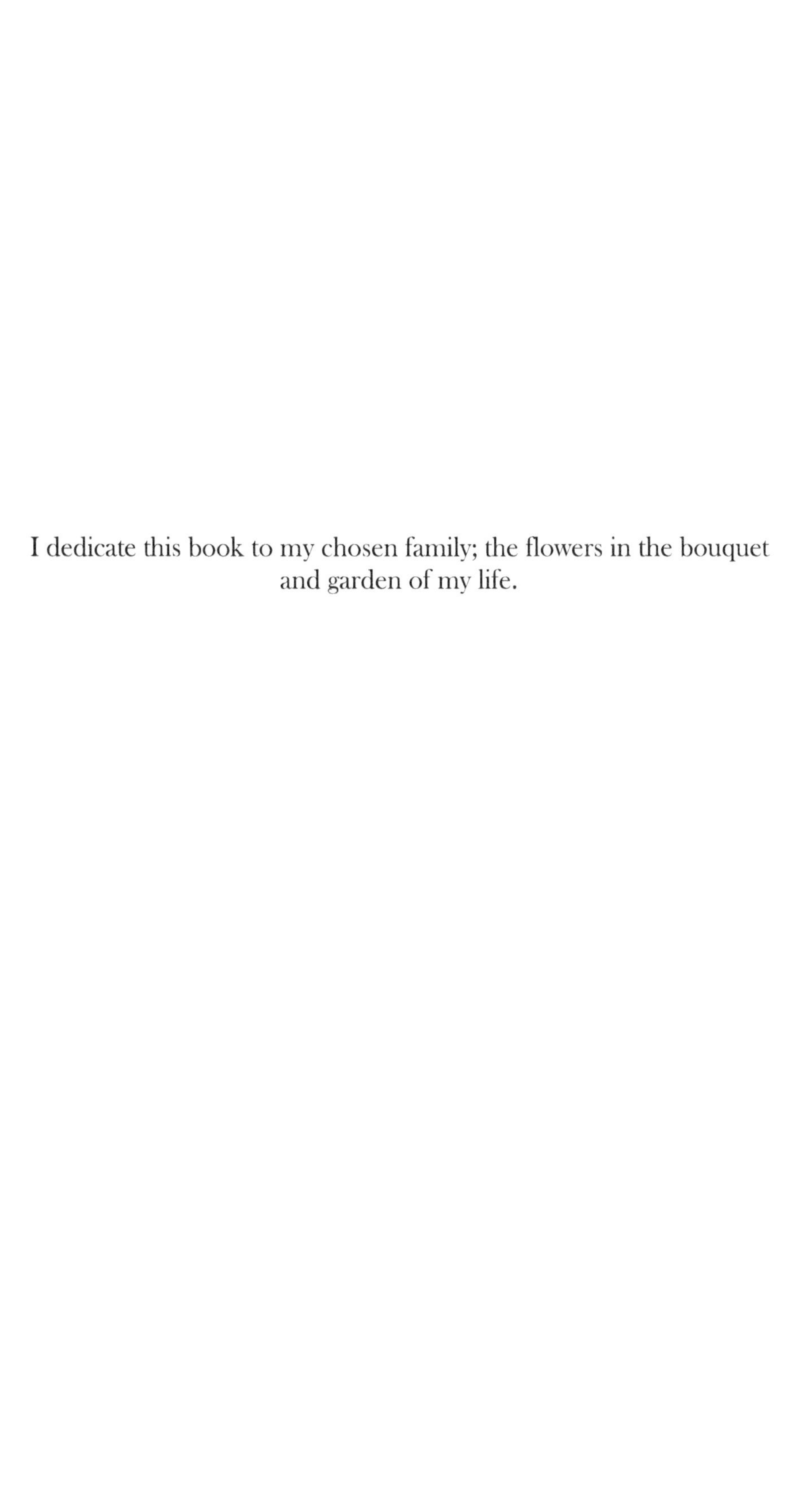

I dedicate this book to my chosen family; the flowers in the bouquet and garden of my life.

ACKNOWLEDGEMENTS

I would like to thank Mr. John A. Hadley, of John A. Hadley Design for his beautiful work on the book jacket. You are a creative genius! Thank you as always, to friends, family, and other inspiring souls around me. Thank you to my social work colleagues and to the field of social work, for supporting our nation during a most challenging year—2020. It is an honor and privilege to be a part of such a selfless profession. I am forever grateful to all the colorful flowers I have picked along the way, whose beauty I celebrate simply for the grace brought to my life.

PROLOGUE

The year 2020 was what I believe to be the biggest social work year many of us in this field have encountered in decades. With it came global pandemic, and an exacerbation of social unrest perpetuated by the ongoing issues of inequality, injustice, and oppression; all of which social workers must help to fight against. Although not the focus of this collection, the gravity and saturation of these issues caused me to reflect on the meaning of my life, my relationships, the lives of my loved ones, my place in the world, and my ability to continue advocating for others, especially those in need.

This collection of poems not only reminds me of the value of all living things, but also of the importance of immersion in moments shared with others that are as unique as they are fleeting. My mother used to say, "Kathy, you collect people like people collect things." She was right. People are the flowers I have picked along my journey; some whose beauty I enjoyed briefly, others who remain in gardens I cultivate, some in bouquets I carry, and others who are rose petals pressed between pages of dusty books. Despite the challenges of 2020, I continued to encounter and collect flowers, while also listening to the stories of the flowers others collected, which I have shared in this collection of poems. I hope that as you read these poems, they remind you to cherish those flowers *you* have picked along the way. For even if they have not remained in your own bouquet or garden, I do hope what they brought to your life enhanced it in a most colorful and special way.

Among the Flowering Weeds...

GOOD NEWS

I was exhausted and suffocated by
Other's "good news" stories
The unrelenting
"So happy for you"
Stated while gargling
Bitter tasting resentment

I *am* happy for you
I love you
And yours
Like my own
Yet my challenges
Are met
Void of the abundance of love
That which makes them appear
Easier to manage

Good news comes for me
In much smaller packaging
I am forced to step away
Despite my joy for you

I'm really quite sorry
I cannot share this with you
Just know
It's best your party
Does not include
The cloud of my discontent

I wish you well
As always

EXHAUSTION

Sometimes
I'm so close to the edge
So tired of standing
With my toes on the ledge
I welcome a push
Hope for a push
That will ensure
The fight is over

It's all uphill
Although
No one ever tells you that
You climb and you climb
Wildflowers you pick along the way
A sandwich in your backpack
The illusion of a peaceful journey
Until a storm hits
A mountain of mud
Inevitable lost footing
Slide to oblivion

When the sun finally rises
A most welcomed visibility
We continue our journey
Hope for the energy
To avoid inertia
Don't rest too long

No one ever talks about the exhaustion
A secret tightly held
Even though we can see it
In each other's eyes

I'm so tired
So tired of this often, futile climb
Looking down at how far I've come
Looking up towards the distance
I have yet to conquer

Just a thought...
Give me a push...will ya?

EQUILIBRIUM

It's complicated
A tangled web
Rubber-band ball
Where a change in one aspect
Disrupts
The barely sustainable
Equilibrium

Get married
Fall in love
In any order
Suddenly to find yourself
Wedged
Disappearing
Into an abyss of expectations
A mapped plan for your life
For which you have little say
If any

I understand the necessity
Of your immersion
Your need to supplement
Break from the mundane
The expected
Hiding in plain site
Desperately trying
To fulfill unmet needs
This persona you have created
To remain in the equilibrium
Keep the house of cards
From falling

Speaking of which
I am falling for you
You likely guessed that
Felt it

And yet, continue to share yourself
With me
Am I helping with your equilibrium?
Or
Am I complicating it further?
Did you anticipate this space?
Or
Are you surprised?
Pleasantly?
Does this affair bring joy?
To your otherwise
Tangled web?

We have landed here
Regardless of our initial motivation
Simply trying to connect
With another
We have found a synchronicity
Quite unexpected
Amazing
So sweet

I wait for the day
You become transparent
Tell all
Show all
All
All
And all
When I may disclose
I have seen you
All along
What then
Will we be

I will understand
As I understand now
Your efforts to maintain
Equilibrium

A.K.A. WHO???

I didn't want to let go
I felt my soul
Untangling
From yours
Knew it would be a process
Anticipated the necessity
Of my departure
From your life

You assured me
With your promotion
Of beginnings
Based in honesty
I wrapped your words around me
A fleece blanket
Felt safe believing
In you

With immediacy
I made offers
Many of which are often discouraged
In the early stages
Of blossoming romantic intimacy
Sadly
I know no other way

The touch of your hand
The kindness in your eyes
A face with expressions
That put me at ease
I placed faith
In that
Quickly gave friendship
Comfort
Intimacy
Openly
Completely

With love in my heart
Ever-evolving
With every visit
Encounter

I moved towards you
You towards me
Our lips inches apart
Until our bodies
Found a space of right
Meant
Still, you withheld
Truth
I searched for every justification
Believed validations
Solely concocted
By my need
Desperate want
To believe in you
Us
This

I'm not simply a place to visit
A body to arouse
A soul to inhabit
I am a person
Deserving of so much more
I am a person who wants
From you
To give to you
Feel the joy of your acceptance
Gratitude
To share with you
Build from this
Ever-burgeoning foundation
Of deep connection
And yet
Omissions of your truth
Border your heart

From me
You
Us
And *this*

I rode along sad today
The belief we could be something
Slowly dissipating
Hope for this
Complicated by every moment
I look into your eyes
Confused by the transparency
Of your affection for me
Albeit not enough
For you to be truthful
Overwhelmed by fear
You'd never tell
Will you?

If you don't
If you don't disclose
Of your own volition
All that I know
Have known
Since the beginning of
The possibility of us
I will say goodbye
Kiss your cheek
Offer my compassion for your predicament
The blindness of your choices
Tragic mistakes
Missteps
And forever
Walk away

A PLACE TO CRY

It's like this internal debate
Do I hold it in
Or let it flow?
In this crowd
Among "others"
Better to display
Preferred
Most sought after
Cheer
Until the last smile
Is so forced
It's painful
Then I know
...I know
It's time to find a place
To cry

Where is it??

GUM

Big wads of gum
Plug the holes in your soul
Frantically run
Cry when it doesn't hold

Struggle your companion
Creativity your guide
Accept what you've been handed
You have nowhere to hide

You're going to see this through
You're going to figure it out
You know what to do
Survival's what you're about

The last time we connected
I wondered if you were intact
Strategies resurrected
You took your life back

Standing tall in the worst
Despite the leaks in your soul
Hollow from thirst
Still plugging the holes

JUMPED

I jumped into your world
Both feet
Eyes wide open
Encountered your flaws
Focused instead
On all that makes you beautiful
Supported you
Through challenges
Found joy
In your favorite activities
Thus
Imagining I could love you

Sounds like a perfect beginning
However
I reach and reach
For you
Just when I believe we've connected
Your heart you withhold
So, I dance around topics
Walk carefully on eggshells
Filter my discussion
Choose words that
Keep waters calm
And I wait for the day
You are in it with me
Both feet
Eyes wide open
Still fearing
I will be forced to let go
When there is nothing left
To hold onto

HEAVEN/HELL

Can you feel it?
Oh, the sun
How it kissed my face
As I stretched my legs
My toes commanding the gravel
The terrain
I was made for this
My body in a dance
With the topography
I am one with God
Nature
The universe
I run!
Mile after mile
Uninhibited
Sweat and salt
Glazing my body
This is my heaven

I'm sorry
What was that acronym you used?
A long walk
A dark corridor
My sentence
Diagnosis
Words muffled
Garbled
Non-existent
To the healthy
Magnificently well

I sat with someone today
Who's only ever known me to be
What I am
Who I am?
"I used to be a runner," I say
Impossible to imagine

With each passing year
Of ever more confinement
To medical equipment
Functioning now
As my legs
My body
While I fight against it defining me

She smiles when I tell her
About running
A wildcat
Fierce and unencumbered
By her expression
I know she cannot see it
Nor believe it
The gleam in my eye dissipates
Wasteful reflection

Where once my feet
Grasped the earth
Harnessed and garnered it
They rest as lifeless extensions of a body
That defied me
Attempted to destroy my spirit
Successful in its quest
To steal what remains of me
My life
This is my hell

*I don't know your heaven or hell...I wish only to understand with
love and compassion for you in my heart.*

I KNEW

...And you told

I exhaled
Breathed easier
Secrets
Drips from a faucet
Splashing in a stainless-steel sink

My patience perplexing
Standing beside your life
My intuition
Subsequent exploration
Investigation
Illuminating the truth
Of it all
All

Waited for you
Hoped you would value me
Just enough to be honest
Afford me the opportunity
To make informed choices

Tonight
It began
I knew
You told

Like a dance
Warmth
Acceptance
Enticement
A bouquet of carefully chosen words
Much you would like to share
Ever so much more I want to hear

It's a start

You will tell me the truth
Decrease the space between us
With every disclosure
Keep me falling, falling, falling for you
Assured of my safety

Please...
Just tell me the rest

IMPLIED

It is implied

Short bursts of romance
Love affairs
Hours, nights, days weeks, months
Relationships-ish
Passionate
Torrid
Trysts
The investment in possibility
This one will stick
I just know it
Or
SO not my person

It is just so sad...Only it's not

So sad they say
Through the lens of long-term
"Successful" relationships
Those serial daters
Still searching for "the one"
Aren't we so lucky
We found it?!

How very exciting for you
Yet
Nothing is perfect
The nights you sit across from your person
Watching TV
Nothing new to look forward to
Your freedom lost
Decades ago
When you signed on for
Forever

Pros and cons...

Where you will lean on your person
I will have to call a friend
My person
One who has demonstrated their commitment
To me
Us
Time after time
Year after year
When things get tough
It will be a friend
Near or far
Who sees me through the worst

Love of my life
Soul mate
Comes in more than just one package
Where some have consistency
I have freedom
Live my life
As I see fit
Completely without restriction

No one's life is perfect
It may be implied
My companion-free existence
Is oh, so sad

Not to worry
There is enough love
In many forms
To go around for us all

...you need only ask

JUST FRIENDS

Right beside you...
An old married couple
Sports on the TV
It's Sunday
I'm paying bills
Wrapped in a blanket

It's a scenario imagined
Pretend
Because we're
Just friends
Having decided not to explore the "more"
Who decided?
When?

Just friends
Visitors
Who make small talk
Try to fill the time with substance
Time together salted with glances
The touch of a hand
Never progressing towards
Or beyond
Imagined attraction?

First chance I've had
To see you
Since forever
Shared my excitement
Reciprocated
Through texts
Chats
Conversations
Crossing all boundaries

In person...***void***

My attempt to discuss
Squelched by humor
Subsequent subject change
No hand holding
No leaning in
Not a single moment
Lips so close
A kiss cannot be resisted

It was wonderful to see you
Yet I am confused
About what I thought *we* wanted
You were there with me
With your provocative statements
Agreement about
Explorations we'd embark upon
In person
None of which occurred
No illusions on my part

I packed my bags
Felt the need to run
Not because I'm not crazy about you
Attracted to you
Initially concerned I might fall for you
For real this time
Wanted to slink away in the night
Embarrassed by the carefully planned
Lace bra and panties
The pedicure
The lotion and perfume
Proving I'd entered the extremely uncomfortable space
Of ridiculousness

I truly had a lovely time
And you were a most perfect host
You made me feel welcomed
Cared for
Appreciated

You seemed to genuinely enjoy
Sharing your home
Sanctuary
With me
I am grateful
Yet sad
Indeed, disappointed
And having to accept
You have no interest in touching me
Pressing your body to mine
Tasting my lips
Even as you lie beside me
In your bed

I will therefore leave you
And until I do
I will simply sit beside you
Count the hours to my departure
Pretend we're an old married couple
Make these last hours tolerable
The sting of "what happened"
The inquiry of "I thought we were..."
The reality of
Just friends

NEVER ENOUGH

There's a death toll in these times of pandemic
I watch it rise
As I navigate this reality
With an optimism
Occasionally
Clouded by fear

It's a rainy day
Makes it easier to sit inside
A cave
Sanctuary
Admittedly
So too does this Vouvray
I'm reminded of driving the Loire Valley countryside
Indeed, the globe I've traveled
Never enough
My mantra for *all* things

Just as easily
As I imagine myself
Driving the backroads of Europe
I can close my eyes
See us,
The look on your face
As you brush the hair
From my eyes

Your expression...
...face...

I look away
The remote possibility
You share my feelings
Excites
And shatters me

You'll never be mine...

I have so much to tell you...

Secrets I hold
Perhaps the kind
That make encumbered lovers
Run
Or stay

Stay

I'm an expert in disguise
Hold all things
Like treasures
In my heart
My apothecary cabinet
Catacombs of my soul

Ocean of secrets
Never to tell

So, what then?
Ride the wave
Go along with the entertainment
We offer
Supplementation of
Each other's lives
"Special friends"
Red hot lovers
Who expect nothing
What *do* you expect?

Please expect something
Please look at me
Like you desperately want
To go back in time
And pick me
Invite me along the journey
Of your life

Where I hug your siblings
Sip tea with your mum
Immerse myself
In your culture
You in mine

I wish you knew me
All of me
I wish you knew
Of my treacherous
Albeit colorful journey
How nights alone with you
Heal me
Feed my passion
For life

I wish that I could open my world to you
And you would see yourself
This world
Us
Through my eyes
You would fall madly in love with me
Yearn for me to belong to you
Kiss you before you sleep
Every morning
As you wake

I'm going to say something to you
Hand you a bag of bricks
Expect you to carry it
Like a down pillow

I...WANT...MORE

Long for it
You
Us
A promise of forever
Because I love you

Have from the beginning
When you kissed and
Danced with me

Out of the bag it goes
This disclosure
A rose with sharp thorns
I...want...more
Yet
I live in a world of reality

After I have closed the door
My body still trembling
Heart still racing
Your scent on my skin
My sheets
I close my eyes
Ease into the reflection of this night
It fills me
Beyond satisfaction

I accept you don't belong to me
Never will
I accept there is no one
Who holds me
Touches me
Knows the curves of my body
As do you
I accept what I must
Yet
It has not been
Nor will it ever be
Enough

NOT IN

Not in a space to say
I love you
Even though
I do
I won't

Not in
Won't get in
Until
You
Let me
In

Dreaded it
The intimacy
Reconnection
Post disconnection
Given recurrent
Palpable
Hurtful
Distance
You maintain
That which I fight to decrease

I'll simply disappear
In your arms
Transcend
To elsewhere
Anywhere
Avoid the sinking
Deeper
Deeper
Into this love

Is this our game?
Your distance
Fuels my disappearance
Feeds your distance?

Why?
When it can be
Amazing
All encompassing
More than hot
Today
I'm out
Not in
Won't get in
Until
You
Let me
In

TIME STAMP

I started to identify the time stamp
On everything
After I learned of the first
Expiration date

When I was a child
Some moments
Experiences
Were paradoxically fleeting and never-ending
What I wanted to last
Ended quickly
What I needed to end
Stop
Lasted forever

With the first death I encountered
I started to realize
Events of life are abrupt
Like a sucker punch
Lightening
Or the clap of thunder

Eventually
I developed a knack for preparation
Stay in the moment
Soak up as much joy as possible
Be grateful
For it all passes
In the blink of an eye

And if you look closely
Peer into each event
Opportunity
Occurrence
With a keen and sharp eye
You will see the time stamp
Onset and expiration

Each event, experience
Indeed, ALL of life
Is stamped
Marked for expiration
The tears of joy and suffering
First and best love
Celebrations
Losses
Moments which, take our breath away

Despite the clarity of memory
A taste, smell
Senses that take us back
Alter our reality
The moment is really gone
Having expired
As everything does

In this life
Maintain an acute awareness
Of the time stamp
The often abrupt
Immediate end
Cherish it all
Take none for granted

Baby's Breath...

FEELS OVER

It feels so over
Is it?
This time
Our time
The best times ever
When I held his little hand
Laughed and danced
With him
Until he became a big
Big
SO Big
BOY

The days of my life
Most cherished
Spent as his mother
When he needed one
Does he still?
I only know I need a son
My precious son
This son who is my world

So, I move towards acceptance
Of the steps he takes
Leaps and bounds
Towards adulthood
I love to watch him flourish
And he does
Yet
I want it back
Want him back
The tired days
When I wished he'd grow up

Never grow up

Now he has
Leaving me only with the memories
Of his tiny hand in mine
His youth
So over
So over
Over

CAKE

Slice you up
Pieces of the best cake
I ever ate
Each part of you
A part of me
As then
As now
As forever
And the ways I learned about beauty
In my loving you

INHABIT

I will inhabit a butterfly
So, you will know I am here
I will come to you
In your sadness
My brightly colored wings
Catching your attention
Reminding you of the beauty
That surrounds you

My little one
I shall never leave your side
Even in my passing
I will find a way to sit beside you
My soul forever tethered to yours
I may be that butterfly
Perhaps a singing bird
A puppy who runs to you
Inhabitation to watch over you
All the days of your life
My beautiful child

ENTERPRISING

He likes the experience of enterprising
That boy
For himself
No shackles
Just the freedom to see what he can create
From what he has in front of him

I know someone just like that
A girl whose first job
Was selling old newspapers
Already read
To unsuspecting apartment dwellers
At the age of 7
A girl who held carnivals
Played all the parts
Made the kids laugh
Assigned work responsibilities
To subordinates
At the age of 9
In a rented yard
While collecting nickels and dimes
Made more valuable
By the strategies used to obtain them

This girl grew up fantasizing
About ways creativity
Could be a bridge to freedom
Happiness
Autonomy
Spent her entire life
Trying to bring it all to fruition
Adopted the mantra
"Die Trying!"

Here he is
This young man
He is cut from my cloth
Woven from my fabric
The expression of my DNA
So strong an influence
Both good and bad

I'm going to do the best I can
To step back
See that his happiness
Indeed
Depends on the absence
Of squelching
My constant hovering
Like a wet blanket
He must navigate through life
Wearing

I'm going to try and try
Because I know how important that freedom is
I know his spirit will slowly die
Without his opportunity
To be the wild butterfly
He is

Off you go my tiny!
Even though I understand
I still must try
To let you fly!

EVERY CRASH AND BURN

What business had I
To bring a life into the world
When I had nothing to offer
Such great lies I did tell myself
Imagining
I was a person with much to give
When I could not be more broken
Held together by glue
I quickly discovered
Was not permanent

No business had I
Was never the daughter
Was never the lover
Was never the wife
Demonstrated to myself
Again, and again
I could look the part in my own mind
But not make desired characteristics
Come to fruition
Instead, I cultivated friendships
I could walk in
My imagined, undamaged self
My glued, taped, makeshift self
People were none the wiser
Then I had you...
Then I failed you...
And was reminded
I had no business bringing a child into the world

Now I get to see it all...
Everything about me that may never improve
Every scar that will never heal
Every shitty choice
Every blunder
Every crash and burn

I know because I'm broken
I don't have much to give
So, I give what I can
Sometimes it comes in a monetary package
Sometimes it comes with caretaking
Always it comes with unconditional love
And a deep desire to be your mother

It will never be enough

I give what I can
Substandard at best
This overcompensation
For every shitty choice
Every blunder
Every crash and burn

And every time I am forced
To face my limitations
I will want to run
Escape
Never come back
It is what I have always done
My modus operandi
While I will never know how to do anything else
For you
Only you
I will turn around
And come right back

CODY

I ate him up like cake
Devoured him
Sewed him to my soul
Wore him
A second skin
An extension of me
Who now walks the world
With my blood in his veins

He is my song
Lyrics of my life
The melody
That keeps me proudly skipping
Snapping my fingers
Joyful
For the one great thing I did
When I gave him life

I love that baby
That thick
Chewy baby
Who navigates life
With the wisdom
I infused
As best I could
And a fine job does he
Offering kindness to others
Living ethically
Responsibly
Lovingly
Oh...he makes me proud!

He will always be
The terms of endearment
Spoken like wind chimes
In my heart

Cody Schmodie
Chooch
Cookie
Cookie cakes
My one true love
My beautiful and precious
Cody

Corpse Flower...

INSERTION/DELETION

I insert people – only to delete them
Into and from
My life
In desperate measures
As one of the isolated
Without family
Because everyone
Has their own

I find the holidays excruciating
A constant
Ceaseless
Reminder
Of what I will never have

I keep trying to rescue people
Those without capacity for love
Because I too
Wish to be rescued
Even though I know
I never will

CHURCH

Did she just say
"Let's throw a few beers back ya'll!"
Guess where I am?
Yep
Surprises me too

People often ask me to join them
At their church
Thus far
It hasn't worked out so well
I always expect I will start on fire
The moment I walk in the door
Although I do not
Inside I feel the friction
The environment of good cheer and simplicity
Fanning the flames
Of "you do not belong here"
And I don't

Inside I'm aware of a brewing implosion
Compounded by the weight
Of the demons I carry
Varying in size
And levels of power
Everything I do
Everywhere I go
I carry them
Like handbags
Luggage
A suit filled with sand
Yet I am mobile
Agile
Unwavering in energy

Dragging all
Appearing light on my feet
Unencumbered
Graceful
Courageous
Who can tell
I
Am indeed
The outlier

Who knows the secret
Behind my hand shake and bright smile
Who among us
Longs to raise the voice
Of their own rebellion
As the rest reach into their pockets
For tithe
"10% of what we earn"
As they allege the Bible reads

So, in the process
Of adjustment
Futile attempts at acclimation
I hear what I want to hear
In the sermon
Even though I know it is likely
No one mentioned beers
This Sunday morning

DATING ADVICE

Throw it back!
Bad fish
She said
Not the one for you
What you see
Just the tip of the iceberg

Cut the cord
Cut it loose
Cut sling load
Shut the door
Close the window
Close the blinds
Ditch
Hang up
Block
Delete
Swipe left
Ghost
Disappear
Bolt
Run!

Vulgar
Obscene
Narcissist
Objectifier
Emotionally unavailable
Dishonest
Deceitful
Predatory
Nothing to offer!
Zilch!

Self-respect
Self-love
Self-compassion
Self-esteem
Self-confidence
Self-efficacy
Dignity
Pride

Love yourself more than another
Love yourself enough
To move on!

DRUNK

I spend my darkest days
Drunk
But only in my head
I lie on a couch
And I don't care
If I've showered
Eaten
Or if the sheets are clean

I let bills
And eviction notices
Pile up at the door
I just don't give a shit

It appears the world
Is moving around me so quickly
People are going places
Meeting these arbitrary benchmarks
Marriage
Kids
Kids in college
Kids get married
Grandparents
All set up to convince others
They are disadvantaged
Failures
For not following the script
While I
Live a life
Of
Fuck all that

I'm going to remember
Remind myself
I was never textbook
I lived a journey
Not an outcome

Talked back
Pushed back
Explored at my leisure
Took some hard blows
Stood back up
Pressed on

I painted my own canvas
In the abstract
Rather than the paint by numbers
Of most

I remember
Remind myself
I owe no explanations
To anyone
My choices
My life
That it's no one's
Goddamn business
What I do
How I've navigated
Or lived this life
Then
I get up
From that stinking ass couch
Shower
Eat
And wash my sheets

So, I can tell you to **fuck off**
When you question my choices
I'm thrilled they are not synchronized
With yours
Or the cookie-cutter life you live
The prescription you followed
To ensure your happiness
Did it?

And when you hear the **roar** of my voice
Feel the **punch** that my flipping you off packs
When I return your judgment
Respond to the unsolicited
Very unnecessary pity on your face
I will sober right up
Every time

THE FISHERY

There you go
All piled high
Slime and sludge
Sickness
Disease
Yet one among you
Will be the delicious find
Treasure

Buckets of fish
In the fishery
My hands soiled
Unavoidable and lingering stench
Inherent in the search
For one
Just one
fine
fish

MONSTERS

Running as fast
As far
As I can
Hoping this obsession
Passion for you
Blows off me
Leaving no trace
Of what I told myself
I had to have

My rebound
Your lips
Skin
Taste
The perfect cocktail
Recipe
Storm

You're dirty
A liar
But so damn pretty
Gifted
Know exactly what to say
How to say it
Ease me into
"I'll do anything"
No effort expended
Or required...

You took me somewhere
I'd never been
Then
I craved
All of you

A delicious taste of salty skin
Devoured
A need for more, MOre, and MORE

Fantasy became reality
The monster appeared
I gagged on the taste
Of your rancid flesh
Clawed out your eyes
Ran for my life

A wretched and rotten sociopath
Wrapped in a cloak of charm
Takes them by the hand
Leads the dance
Captivates them
Until tired and bored

Eventually seen for what they are
Monsters
With whatever remains intact
We run
Not without injury
Bruising
Scars
And perhaps the best life lessons
Yet

NARCISSISM AND SOCIOPATHY

Blows in
A gust of hot wind
I'm suddenly uncomfortable
No space lends to ease
I'm suffocated
By let downs
Lack of accountability
The misfortune of having crossed paths
With persons of compromised character

They're out there
They walk among us
Blinded to the needs of others
By illusion of love for themselves
A true overcompensation
For hollowed existence
Soullessness
A special and toxic blend
Of narcissism and sociopathy
They are a plague
That destroys all around them

OUTCOMES

Sometimes
The chains rattle
So loudly
I am paralyzed with fear
The shackles
Of choices
Shiny and polished
Rusted on the inside
Am I ever going to get it right?

You're going to have your holidays
You'll hold hands
Laughter wafting with blends of spices
Pride in all you've created
Cultivated

I will hang on
Barely
Until I find the footing
Of my survival

Trouble
Mischievous
Darkness
Bitter
High
Drunk
Whore
The best liar you ever met
The best liar I ever met
The necessity of such lies
All for the outcomes

What of the lies
How did it turn out?
You fucked it up
Grandly
Told yourself you were something you're not
Never will be
Tried to become one of
The "blessed"

Dress up in business casual
Attach degrees to a name
Fill your mouth with fancy words
String them together in sophisticated sentences

Go home to your temporary and empty space
Scrub the makeup off your face
Throw your imposter-wear on the floor
See yourself for who you are
Unworthy
Unloved
Crouching in a corner
Covering your ears
Blocking out the bang
And blasts
Of failure
Choices made
Outcomes that reinforce
It can't be taught

You will always be how you began
Dirt on your face
A scent about you
You'll never scrub clean

They'll say you tried
But trying is not valued
Even though they say it is
No matter the strategies you employ
The outcomes are always the same

Never a winner
Not on this day
Not at this time
Not in this life
Despite the desperation
To change the outcomes

FUCK!

PATHETIC

...I'm not

My poorest decisions
A fishnet over my life
Effects my mobility
Yet, I am not
Nor will I ever be
Without the resources
Resiliency
To manage
Persevere
Through any outcome
Eventually
Tearing a hole through the net

I hate the sound and look
Of disappointment
Your sighs
Expression
As I mistakenly
Spray your face with disclosure
Imagining my having spared you the details
Sharing only the outcome
Would be much easier for you
To reconcile
Digest

Yep!
Fucked up again
It is what it is

I am not interested in approval
Have lived my life entirely on my own
Not needed anyone to support me
Despite gratitude
Appreciation
When it happens

No
I won't seek your approval today
As in that process
Inevitably
I confront self-doubt
Suffocating disgust in myself

Instead
I'll spare you
And me
By withholding details, outcomes
All truth
My truth
Display a seamless life
Of celebrated choices
Expert in disguise

It's hard to love me
Isn't it?
The elegance and sophistication
In my creation of catastrophe
When ironically
I seek nothing more or less
Than any other
Love, kindness, honesty, loyalty...
All that makes us humans thrive

My decisions and strategies
The best intentions
Over estimation of integrity in others
Leading me to the same end
Mistakes
Missteps
Undeserved or earned trust
Given freely
In love

I'm trying
I say
This *is* my best
The slack I cut
The wrong people
Always
Leaves me standing
In a heaping pile of shit
I
More than you, or any other
Am acutely aware

Did it again

You're tempted to judge my choices
They are after all
Judge-worthy
It's enticing
A head scratcher
"Why would you ever...?"
All notions and curiosities
Justified

Know
I pose the same questions to myself
Exhaustive inquiries and analysis
Certainly
That is enough

I'm not going to burden you further
Spare you the details
Strategies I employ
Simply to meet my needs
Love
Live
In my way

When it's all said and done
When I dust off the dirt
Scrub my body clean of the filth
The unavoidable stains
Of my poor choices
We'll talk
And I'll retrieve my stock responses
Just for you
Me
I'll be fine
I'm fine
Oh that? It just didn't work out

PERFECT LOVE/ILLUSION

I'll say goodbye to you
My words couched
In a kind of love and support
For which you have no frame of reference
Though, I owe you
Absolutely nothing

Your desire for me
Confused by your desperate need
For the illusion of perfect love
Held me
This
Us
Accountable
For all which remains unresolved
In the chaos
That is your life
A healing that your opportunistic soul
Longs for

I understood
Accepted goodbye
No choice
You could no longer maintain
The façade
Of loving me
As with all other props
In your life
No longer continue
In the drudgery
Maintenance of the illusion
Of non-existent
Perfect love

So, you are on to the next
Opportunity/victim

I stand in the shadows
Knowing the shelf-life
Of what you offer
Is significantly limited
Expires
Molds like bread
Left out on a kitchen counter
In humid, summer heat

Ever so sorry for the current soul
Who has now crossed
Your destructive
Reckless path

SIDELINES

Vanity
Self-loathing
Or both
It keeps me on the sidelines
Side
Lines
Where...

Where I say
FUCK IT
And THIS
Never was the outdoorsy type
Especially now
When years have been unkind
I'm in the saturation of poor choices

Join us you say
I hate that word
I'm not a joiner
Not a joiner
I don't have her, his, or your freedom
I have my imperfect body
A mind that plays tricks on me
Circles above my confidence
Like a vulture
Carefully planning attack
It's not simply vanity
Self-loathing
It is the residue of dysmorphia
A plague
That makes the small steps of joining
Daunting

For today
I'll watch
From the sidelines
Of something barely appealing
I'm fine here
Sweating
Waiting
Until the day ends
In my vanity
Self-loathing
And within my obsessive mind
It is my burden to bear
Torture to endure
Confinement

TURN

A sharp turn
Painful whiplash
Didn't see it coming
Or maybe I did
Ignored it
In favor of hope
Fog with a purpose
Clouded perception

Maybe this time?

The person who sashays through the room
With toilet paper on their shoe
The person who smiles brightly
With lettuce in their teeth
The person who is called out as winner
And told later
A mistake has been made

We all strive to present our best selves
Try to hide when we cannot
A careful and strategic concealment
That only brings relief with the illusion
Inadequacies have gone unnoticed

I hoped today
I hoped for purpose and relevance
I hoped a most futile hope
It fell away
Under a heavy tarp of isolation

WRECKING BALL

Words like a wrecking ball
Didn't
Don't
See coming

I thought we could finally move on
All your dirty deeds
Behind us

Here we are
Yet again
You find an opportunity
To remind me
Of deceit
That has left scars on the heart that loves you still

It will never be funny
Entertaining
Jokes about women you fucked
As you fed me the lies
Of your love and commitment
A taste once sweet, rich like frosting
Turned bitter
Putrid
Time nor distance make your indiscretions
Laughable
Forever they are the stains we can cover
Yet never remove

Each passing year
I hope will be the last
You will ever bring that shit up again

And then
Without fail
The wrecking ball

YOUR FANTASY UNTIL

I'm not your fucking church girl
But
I can be
Your girl

I can be your angel
Spin round you
Like twilight
In a dream-like state
And when you need
A dirty girl
I will transform
Until your every fantasy
Is reality
Just...the way...you...like it

I can be whatever you need
A shoulder to cry on
Stability
Footing
You never knew possible

My willingness to please you
Is boundless
Until the moment
You take it/me
For granted

Then your fantasy
Lover
Most cherished companion
Damn dirty girl
Who signed on for any
And all
Walks away

Deuces mother fucker!

OUTSIDE

...Sometimes
Looking in

You're always going to be on the outside
Of all things inside
When the party includes the celebrated
Connected
When the clique has all of those in the circle
When the entrance is cleared
For those who would have the honor of invitation
You are not
Nor will you ever be
In the space
That feels like home

For you
There is no home
You wander about
A fantasy of inclusion
Questioning your true interest
In belonging
Peering through the broad hues
Of stained glass
Imagining
It could be you
It could be me
It could be us
It is not

Instead
You are on the other end
Behind it
The outside
...Sometimes
Looking in

DESPERATION

The desperation of a loved one or a person in need, makes us inclined to help

A stranger's desperation, or a person we're not really into, makes us feel like we've accidentally brushed against someone's sweaty skin at the gym

A narcissist's desperation makes us feel like we're shoveling snow while it's still snowing

Your desperation feeds the narcissist, and is the fuel they need to continue victimizing you

Lilies and Goodbyes...

ENDED HERE

And what if she did it
She just hung from somewhere
Over something
A sad sack
Whose light simply went out

What if she
Let go
Ended
Who would cry for her
For ten minutes
Or more

Just that, please
Just cry
Remain silent
Remember her bright light
Despite the dimness
That followed

She fought hard
With a fierceness
No one could sustain
Eventually
All energy ceases
Hers...
It ended *here*

PATHS

They awoke in each other's arms
Blissful fog
A long night of lovemaking
Deepened bond

I see them on the hiking trail
She in her bike shorts
Perfect figure
His beaming smile
Whenever he looks at her

I take a different path

A twinge of resentment
A slight bit of envy
Until I remember
I had that once
With you

We'd make love into the night
Cuddle and laugh
Go to the gym together
Weekend trips

People looked at us
A slight bit of envy
Twinge of resentment

I thought you loved me
Believed you
When you said you did

You took a different path

It didn't kill me, you know
I don't lie awake
Wondering
What went wrong

I imagine your life
Scripted
A systematic blending
Of activities
Each day identical
To the one before
To the one that follows

The end of us
Forcing me to imagine
A new route on my journey
And while yours is now determined
By another

I create my own path

BE IN IT

The most beautiful thing you will ever see
Life
As it exits the body

If you can briefly suspend
Pain of loss
You will experience tranquility
In the stillness
Of a transitioning soul

Your own soul will reconcile
Where ever the soul of the person
Drifts
Is a place we all go
Someday
Trust in a glorious outcome
Of a long or short journey
Struggle
Pain, suffering
Joy
Ending with a shift in palpable energy
For those present
When a loved one passes

Temporarily
Move from your sorrow
You'll have plenty of time for that
Be present for this fleeting gift
Of peace
As your loved one releases
Their grip
On physical life
Embrace its inevitability
Celebrate that you had this glimpse
That some may never have

Only those of us whom have witnessed
The passing of a loved one
Held in our hearts this miracle
If we indeed allowed ourselves
Just one moment
To be in it

BILLY BOY

There's something so awful about it
Excruciating
Pain for which
There is no relief

So pretty
A baby, joy in his smile
I held his face
In my hands

See him?
He's eight years old
All his tiny bones
Standing there to tell the truth
An honest baby
Hold you
Kiss you
Love you
Until you vanish
Powder
Dust that blows away
With darkness
A gust of wind
POOF!
Gone

I look at that picture
A man whose beaming smile
Lights up every room he enters
Lit up every room he entered

Where did you go
Precious boy
Not my own
Not of my womb

Yet loved me
And I him
As if he were mine

Sometimes
I can't breathe
When I feel the rubber band snap
On soft skin
A sting
Pierce
Reminding me
You're gone forever

I want to kick a huge hole in the wall
Because you disappeared
When I thought you'd be here forever
I can't say goodbye to you
Won't
Because Aunties don't outlive
The babies they hold
And I did this time
And it's my knife
The stab wound
I will have
In my heart forever

COCHEM ON THE MOSELLE

Wine, cheese, and bread
A slow dance
Cochem on the Moselle River
Light breeze
Summer day
Hoped you loved me still

Took your hand
Led you in a dance
Held your body to mine
Ja
You loved me still

Weekend of superficial romance
Convincing me
We were "us" again
A tragic mistake

Summer sunshine
Overshadowed by darkness cast
Love lost
Forever
Romance conjured in desperation
Futile

Exotic places are like duct tape
Stuck it on
Patched the holes
The seams burst anyway
Blew up in my face

It was over
The moment you said goodbye
The first time
Only I didn't know it
Yet

When I listen to songs
That remind me of that day
My cheek pressed to yours
Your hand in mine
I remember the finality
Last attempt to salvage
Mit
Wein, käse, und brot
Ein langsamer tanz
Cochem on the Moselle River

DIVORCE

Time to let go
Let...it...go

Every time
I no longer see myself
In this relationship
I know it's time to move on
And I do
I move on just enough
To maintain the basis
Of how and why
We came together in the first place

New place
Change of venue
Something to carry me
Through the next chapter
Maintenance of the illusion
Of "we're not the same"
If not together

I am not the same
When we **are** together
Morph into an institutionalized version
Of myself
Whose inner light
Slowly dims
And before the death
Final flicker
I change the venue
Again

Here we are
Over twenty years in
The dreams I had
Are now the reconciliation
Of the reality

The "just enough"
Of having made a difference *sometimes*
Here and there
With some
Yet not all
Right?!

I take care of myself
Despite constraints
Stretch and spread my wings
Even when clipped
By circumstances
Beyond my control
My spirit now and always
Driving my interest
In seeing this through
To whatever end is planned
By the universe

I'm going to go one day
Let go
Only on occasion
Will I permit myself to reflect
On the reasons
I remained
In it
For those remarkable moments
Of nurturing
Love
And growth

I will have little regret
Having made the most
Of every inevitability
That wrapped around me
Sometimes like coarse rope
Chains

I did what I was meant to do
Loved with everything I had
Accepted moments of suffering
With as much dignity and grace
As I could muster
Celebrated multiple ways
My life was enriched
Just by virtue of this relationship

Let it go
Let go
As I know one day I must
Let it all go
Divorce myself
From something that
In many ways
Defines me
Say goodbye to the practice
The field
The part of my soul
Known as social worker

SEE YOU ON THE OTHER SIDE

Here it comes...
I start running
It's too fast now
Faster than ever
No way out of *this* room

Thank you for telling me
Including me
In the planning
Of your final days
An honor I don't deserve

I reflected on times
When we were young
In love
In a place where our choices intersected

Grungy motels
Cable TV
Pizza for breakfast
You made love to me
With your passionate style
No one existed but us
In a world
Contrasted by too much responsibility
For some so young

Although we said a sad good bye
Stretched across years of silence
I missed you still

When timing permitted
At least a decade of lessons past
I looked for you
Was thrilled to find you willing
To give us another try

Even though the flame remained
Our differences illuminated
The need for separate paths

In the decades that followed
You found another
To give you the life and love
You truly deserved
And I found peace
Knowing you were loved
Treasured
On your journey
Living a life
That held
Your deepest desires

All along
My only hope
Was that you would find someone
Who loved you
In ways that I could not

I loved you in my way
Hoped it was enough
Especially now
As I pray
It is enough

Goodbye my love
I cannot hold your tired hand
Nor kiss your cheek
Yet
You know I love you
Will miss you
And will see you on the other side

FENTANYL

I'm on the Fentanyl plan
It's going to help me decide
When to hang it up
It's the how
Of the why
It will follow the time I trip
Scrape my face on the sidewalk
Break a bone or two
The poor prognosis
No hope for a sad sack like that
Just a few crumbs
The suffering ends
The constant face in the mirror
Pointing
Laughing
Dumbass

Well fuck you!
I'm done with it all
Down she goes with a glass of Belvedere
More refreshing
Than this shithole life

I will disappear
After this final act
An end
To end
This inevitable
Sink

ENDS HERE

I pressed my hands
Against the glass
...I'd climb out and roll onto the highway
If I could
Because I could fall madly for you
Your hair
Smell
Taste
Because you're smart
Precious
Fun
And temporary
Because it ends here
Now
Tonight

I hate it...
I hate it...
Hate that it ends here

MY PEACE

A man who once beat me
Mercilessly
Died today

For him
I never held ill will
Never dragged a bag
Of pity or pain
With his name on it
And yet
Suddenly
The earth has more space
For me to roam
Freely
Now that he
Is no longer on it

With the death of every person
Who victimized me
My heart and soul heal
Just a bit more
The loss of whom some will mourn
My peace

FORK

She's gone
I say her name in a whisper
Louder hurts more
The hard words
Spoken softly
Because a scream packs a mean ass punch

I danced to your favorite song yesterday
Spun around
Like when we were girls
Remembering the joy
In our dances
Jokes and laughter
Hope filled dreams
Plans for growing old

I'm still here
Walking the earth
Living for both of us
Never forgetting
How much adventure
Dances
Jokes
Just plain living
Meant to us

I waved goodbye to you
At the fork in the road
No choice
Trusted I'd see you
On the other side

Tonight
Memory colored dances
Us
Glamming it up
Streets of Chicago
The promise
Of tired decades of adulthood
Ahead
Until
...the fucking fork

For my sister Andrea, who I kissed goodbye at the fork...

LIFE OF MISSING

Isn't it a life of missing?
Missing loved ones
Missing what we once held dear
Cherished
Youth
Innocence
Naivete
Like a garden of wildflowers

Desperately
We shift our focus
To the attainable
Accessible
Reachable
That which we may grasp
Hold tightly
Until the time
It is forced from our grip
Yanked away
While we cry
Beg
Scream
Arms and hands extended
As something we love
Transitions to something
Terribly
Terribly
Missed

Acceptance of the inevitable
For there is no other recourse

What then
Makes it manageable
The holding on
Releasing
And missing

It is the joy
Of being in it
The soulful immersion
Loving what we have
When and while
We have it

I'm never going to get used to it
Despite the multitude of ways
I engage this experience
I feverishly try
Holding on to what I know
Is always temporary
Fleeting
Momentary
Because I love it so damn much

Such is life
A lifetime of goodbye(s)
And missing

PARTY ON THE OTHER SIDE

Hour of death
Day
Year
Decade
Decades
Dozens
Depart
One after the next
Along with pieces
Parts
Of me

I wait
And whither
More
With each loss
Until the transition
To the party
On the other side
Where dozens
Wait to greet me
Where my soul
Reconstitutes
Heals

A party indeed
Soul's hello
Celebration
End of earthly existence
The gift of love
Enveloping

ONE MORE TIME

I was going to sit in the window
Watch one more bird fly
One more bee land
On the flowers in the garden

I was going to tell each person
Who saved me
Thank you
Just one more time

I was going to stay in a fancy hotel
Get all dressed up
Dinner and dancing
Feel like a queen
Just one more night
Just one more

I was going to make love all night long
Scream your name
A wide smile
When you screamed mine
It was going to be hot and sweaty
Like many before
Yet this time, it would be our last

I was going to hold hands
With the nieces and nephews
For whom the gift of watching them grow
Loving them
Has been a most profound experience

I was going to kiss my boy
My treasure
Jewel
My heart
The love of my life
Kiss his cheek
Smell his skin
Nestle my head against his chest
Hold him as tightly as I could
Just one more time
One more time

Instead
I stayed on the track of "day to day"
Imagining it was the right choice
After all, there are so few breaks
Working, toiling
A loathsome grind
I thought I would outlive

In the mindset of just a bit longer
I missed my chances
To say and do what matters
The most
And when the day came
I would receive the news
Of impending death
I scurried and failed
To do it all
Just one more time

SADDENED

Saddened
Sadd ened
Sad end

I will curl up
On a plush sofa
Cloud
Write about how I once loved you
Love you still
Recall how hard
You tried to love me

Holding my hope tightly
Against my heart
Each of your kind gestures
Expressions of your feelings for me
Fanned the embers
Of our synchronized passion

We were almost there
Weren't we?
What was in your eyes
More real for me
Than words can explain
Until you walked away
Left me saddened
By our
Sad end

PICK ME

I fell in love for the last time
The last time I fell in love

Was it?

Maybe

You danced with me
Along the side of the road in Tuscany
Remember that?
I should have known
By how closely you held me
You anticipated the end
Now every time I hear that song
I'm there
Right there
And I miss you

You didn't pick me

Thought you would

All these years later
I wonder what it might have been
To kiss you goodnight
Wake beside you each morning
To count on you
As we trekked along the journey
Of life
For every skinned knee
A band-aid
Every tear shed
Wiped by a hand
That held mine
In the hard stuff
Of life

I wasn't your person

I guess

Even though we laughed
Uncontrollably
Danced with passion
Loved with commitment
Excited by possibility
Where there was really
None at all

Who knew?

You did

I'll listen to that song
Forever
Mostly because I love
The haunting lyrics
The melody

Whenever I hear it
I'll see us again
Dancing along the side of the road
In Tuscany
Perhaps I'll have a moment
When I'll wish
You'd *picked me*

PRECIOUS, TINY BOY

...just a boy
Did you know him?
He came to me
Wanted to know
How
When
Where
Who
Wanted to know how the world spun
Decide between winners and losers
Wanted to understand his path

Despite my decades ahead of him
I had so few answers
Searched my heart
Soul
Offered wisdom
To his satisfaction
To me...*never enough*

Saturday afternoon
Took a call
His lifeless body
Found without resemblance
Of all things
That made him beautiful

He was once a precious
Tiny
Boy
Grew into an introspective soul
Man with 1000 questions
Inquiries
Ponderings
A finely sharpened ability
To analyze

So dear to me
How I enjoyed
Appreciated
Our philosophical
Critical
Conversations
When bestowing my wisdom
Was but a small token
Of my love for him

I miss you
I missed imagining you
All grown up
Sharing wisdom
I passed to you
With your own daughters

I missed the opportunity
For you to hold
My wrinkled, aged hand
Tell me stories
Comforted by the relief of knowing
It all turned out okay
It didn't

Precious
Tiny
Boy
Tender young man
Loving
Bleeding heart

Faster than I could say
I love you
He was gone

For Billy, who is missed still...

RISE

I didn't wake this morning
Well sort of
I transcended to another realm
Saw my lifeless body
Wondered what led to my demise
Did me in

Oddly I felt no regret
I reflected on my life
Rife with tragedy
Palpable pain
And with each smash of the hammer
The sun still rose
Cast brightness across my suffering
Illuminated possibility
Infused deep within me
The determination I needed to fight
Another day

It was a life well-lived
Countless opportunities to recognize and celebrate
The beauty and joy in *all*
Even through moments
I was certain would kill me

My mother's descent into Alzheimer's
Watching her disappear
Yet, paving the agony of her trajectory
With music
Stories
Pictures
Touching her beautiful face
Her eyes still smiling

The end of my brother's life
And in many ways
My own
On a cold winter night
Yet forever
I would have the memory
Of dancing with him for my sweet sixteen

My sister's last breath
A sword through my heart
Softened by decades
Of laughter
Dancing
Sisterhood
That would carry me through the remainder
Of my life

Rape
Molestation
Assault
Overdose
Sickness
Heartbreak
Murder
Goodbyes
Mine, yours, ours
All necessary
To ensure the celebration of sunlight
Acceptance
The gratitude that cultivates true happiness
In the face of all adversity

It was worth it
All of it
It was worth it
To be dragged
By my hair

To lie in a heap
Slowly stand
Find my footing
Throw my fists in the air
And shout ENOUGH!
It was worth it
To fall in love
Make love
Many nights of romance
Lover's hearts
I penetrated
Passion tattooing my soul
With color

It was worth it
Emotional, spiritual, physical paralysis
The process through which I regained
Movement
Assuring an unwavering belief
In myself

It was all worth it
Even though this morning
I didn't wake
Wasn't aware last night
Was indeed my last

Yes
The energy of my soul
Fueled my desire for adventure
I lived as some never do
And as my time has come
To transcend
My soul is content
In its final reflection

YOU'LL BE FINE

I missed my mother today
A conversation about my life
I needed to have
Advice I was seeking
A smile that assured me
Everything will be okay
I missed her
Because it was her job to care
Did it well
Allowed me to lead her into that role
When she was simply too exhausted

Yes, I miss her
My guide in the navigation
Of unpredictable topography
Through fear
Or the sharing of joy
A true friend
Whose love was a source of energy
That gave me the strength to keep going
What about now?
What propels me forward
Sells me on the notion of "one more try"
It is knowing I was loved
For as long as she could love
As much as she could love
The times when I said
What will I do when you're gone?
I won't be able to do this
To which she would reply
You'll be fine...
You'll see
You'll be fine

Just as you predicted momma, I'm fine.

SILVER

So handsome
With your smooth olive skin
Still concealing
The multiple obstacles
Of life
After all this time
The only telltale sign
Head of silver

So handsome
Funny
Animated
Fills a room
With laughter

We are all aging
Transitioning
From one phase of life
To the next
With grace
Patience
Which comes only
With wisdom gained
Through life experiences

I see him
As clearly as if
He stands before me
His beautiful face
Silver hair
Beaming smile

He is only an image
He never really aged
Taken at 23

All I ever wanted
Was to grow old with him
I fight to create the image
Of what might have been
How we'd poke fun
At each other's old faces
Wrinkles earned
Celebrated
Evidence of trials
Survived

Instead
It's lonely
Growing old
Without you

For just enough
To remember
Just enough
To remember you
I'll imagine your handsome
Yet wrinkled face
Smile that made everything better
Shiny, silver hair
The image is my peace
What could have
Should have been

There is comfort knowing
I will see you again
The day when my own head of silver
Rests against my pillow
As I draw my last breath
Like me, you too
Will have been waiting

*For my brother Bill, who was everything to me; he is missed the
same every day, every year, every decade...*

DEPARTURE

In a moment
While I walked carefree
Along the beach
You took your last breath

When the sun set
I washed the sand and salt
From my hair
As you lie frozen
Undiscovered

A much-needed break
From the chaos
Of your addiction
I hoped the time away
Would give us both
The clarity we needed
To decide our next steps
I was determined to leave you
Were I to shed
Just one more tear

The outside of our storm
The space necessary for recalibration
Critical reprieve
From the excruciating pain
Of deep wounds
My life saved
By my temporary
Departure

Red and pink hearts
No valentine had I
Yet
I was certain my return
Willingness to show up
Tag back in

Would mean so much more to you
Than candy hearts
Or a greeting card
Portraying someone else's story

Surprise!
I'm home
Your room
An empty space
I stand still
Suffocated by the void of your sweetness
The energy of love we shared
Siphoned by your death
A bed where once
Endless hours of lovemaking
Now the tomb
Where your body grew cold

Nothing left
But to take my belongings
Smell your shirts
One last time

Almost 40 years ago
I was a girl
Excited about Valentine's Day
And a fresh start
With a person
Who meant the world to me
Instead
I was shattered

Every Valentine's since
I reflect on how deeply I loved you
Miss you still
Until I see you again
Happy Valentine's Day

For B.D.L... If only...

THANK YOU...GOODBYE

Out the door
He walks
Turns back
One last smile
He's a sparkly eyed fella
Indeed

No point in chasing him
Trying to stop him
Urging him to stay

He's leaving the earth
Transitioning
Passport stamped
With cancer

Did you know I needed you to stay
Right here
Somewhere
Anywhere

I could count on your presence
The confirmation
I was once a girl in my 20s
Who fell...*so hard*...for you
Laughed...*so hard*...with you
Made love to you...*breathlessly*
Jumped on many a motel bed
A cooler of beers
And mediocre pizza

You hold a chapter of my life
In your heart
Allow me to access it
Through a portal
Where I see us laughing and dancing
No cares in the world

Although we were not meant
Our love for each other has transcended
Decades
We have found ways to stay connected
Through life's challenges
Loves and losses
Today
I'm leaning into the possibility
Probability
Inevitability
You will depart the earth
An unshakable spirit
Joyful heart
Treasured soul
That will leave
A deteriorating body
Behind

I love you
Want you to know
And have thankfully said it
More times than I can count

If/*when* you go
You will take a part of that girl with you
The one from the 80's
Who will remember us that way
Relive us that way
Love you that way
Always

WENT ON

It went on
Forward
Life
Despite the injustice
Imbalance
In what I offered
Received
It simply went
On

Images of you
Content
Leave me to question
The accountability
Of it all
If any

Resentment
Deeply grounded
In disappointment
In myself
I knew better
Tried anyway
Knew that you
Would never give me
What I wanted
Still
I hoped
The unconditional love
I offered
Would inspire a reciprocity
That would connect us
All the days of our lives
It didn't
And life
Went
On

I try to understand
Make sense of everything
That happened
Sad
When I imagine
I meant so little to you
At peace when I realize
You gave me what you could
Convinced
It would never have been
Enough for me

It is the justice
I have long sought
To see you with another
Appearing content
I know in my soul
It is exactly as it should be
Because I deserved more
Than the compromised dose
Of your version of love
Grounded in deceit
Betrayal...*the worst*

Unfortunate moments
When our vision of one another's soul
Was clouded by the smoke
Of a love
We thought would carry us through
Any and all storms
It didn't
And when that smoke cleared
I saw you for who you are

Today
Someone else
Basks in how they imagine
Perceive you
As I once did

For a moment it stings
Catches me off guard
Especially when I reminisce
About times
We seemed happy
An illusion
I periodically welcome

When the pain subsides
As it always does
Will
I say to myself
Yes, life has gone on
Without you
Or the fantasy of
Us
And gratefully
I am all the better for it

Rose Garden...

ALL I WANT TO DO IS LIE BESIDE THAT MAN

I didn't know you existed
Three weeks ago
Now all I want to do
Is lie beside you
Feel your body against mine

I hate the way I look right now
Sick in bed
Trying to heal
And all I can think about
Is lying beside you
Touching your face
Looking into your eyes

Who are you?
You're *someone* to me now
Out of nowhere
You arrived
Crashed into my life
Flipped it upside down
And when I caught my breath
I sunk into you

Now I wait for you to arrive
Give me what I desperately want
What I crave
Just to lie beside that man

COLLECTIVE TRAUMA

In collective trauma
We stand alone in our grief
Present for others
Yet in the stillness
Of how we cope individually

I will hold your hand in mine
You'll rest your head on my shoulder
Leaning into one another
Enough connection
Enough love
Despite the palpable presence of inevitable isolation
It is the way
Our human way

CRAZY

Special brand
Of crazy
Gels with mine
Makes me laugh
Not shy
Nor inhibited
Zero fucks given
Refreshing as it is
Entertaining
Your brand

Wanna laugh
Dance
With a spirit
That attracts
Summons me
So, I do
I play with you
Like we're kids
Because I love
Love, love
Your special brand
Of crazy

DELICIOUS

Delicious
Succulent
Sinking my teeth in
Juice paints my chin
Sweetness I longed and looked for
Rich chocolate pudding

I'm young again
With you
You take me there
Laughter
Depth
Romance

Looked around for a sweetness
Thought I'd never find
Until you

FREEDOM

Please see me
As the epitome of freedom
I am indeed free
Wish to take you into this space
Watch you flourish
Thrive

Initially
You will seem tentative
Confused and lost
In the unfamiliarity
Of your surroundings

Slowly
You will ease into the acceptance
Of the sacrifices one must make
To exist here
I will be your tour guide
As I have been free
For decades

I will take your hand
Help you navigate
Eventually
You will look into my eyes
Gratitude you have never known
You will get to know yourself
In a light
You never knew possible
And in this realm
We will dance
Laugh
Make love
For as long as we so desire

HOPE

I'll hold hope
Just for you
As much as you need
Want
Hand it back
Small enough doses
To fit into
The desperate hand
Extended
Too tired
Pained
To hold their own
Or receive an amount greater
Than what may fit
Into the palms of hands
Wrung
Gnarled
From fending tragedy

DESERVED/OWED

I had everything in this life
The universe owed me none of it
Perhaps I deserved as much happiness
As most others
Yet
I had it all

I birthed a precious boy
Whose eyes capture sunshine
Sparkles that change me
Every time he looks at me

I saw the most amazing places
Gems
All around the world
Met people with lives
Vastly different from mine
Though they each helped me understand ways
We are all the same

I made love in magical and enchanting places
With people who filled my heart and soul
With magnetic passion
Even when brief
Our connection was always enough
To bring me closer
To my true authentic self

I loved deeply
And was loved by people
Who radiate color
We shared and share something true
Which forever shapes
The best parts of me

Indeed
I had more than I ever deserved
None of which was owed to me

I spend this lifetime in unwavering gratitude
In firm belief
None of my experiences were based in blessing
Achievement
Or superior choices

Instead, it was all for the cultivation of gratitude
That which I share
Daily
With those who may never have
What I have/had

I give of myself freely
To those in need
A touch of human kindness
Feeds my soul
Ensures my expression of gratitude

Such gifts I receive and received
I deserved no more than any other
And the universe owed me
None of it

INDIFFERENCE

There is safety in indifference
Until word and deed
Swing the pendulum
Towards certainty

You walked towards me
Handsome
Smiled
Your energy providing an immediate
Soothing connection
Leaning into our first hello
The first taste of my attraction to you
Still grounded was I
In indifference

The stories you told
Glimpses into your life
A world you painted clearly enough
For me to know you in it
Felt casual
Too easy
Thus, starting a slow
Yet palpable swing
Towards a space I'd come to fear

The illusion of manageable
Began to crumble
With our first dance
...Your body against mine
I sunk into you
The strength of your arms around me
Hand on the small of my back
A familiar fit
Like the déjà vu of our first phone conversation

Still
I denied the pendulum swing
Believed myself to be inert
Frozen in a state of
Indifference
Until your lips met mine for the first time

...sigh...

As the room was spinning
The question "what's happening"
Flooding my mind
Your mouth and touch
Home to me
I chose to deny
The burgeoning clarity
Of that reality

...ah...

We made love with a passion
Representative of years
Of careful exploration
Despite having only known each other
One day
Tried as I might
I could not resist
The drift
The sway
Undulation
That would swing that pendulum
Further
With each wave
Of our synchronized hips
Yet
I kept my distance...
Held a shield over my heart
And with each word
My protection crumbled

Evidence of my visibility
Overwhelming

We said goodbye
My expectations low
Fleeting passion
As the morning light would illuminate
Then your call
When you circled back around
My shield seemed much less necessary
I trusted you
Your friendship
The words you'd carefully chosen
To build with me
What I have not had the patience
Nor time
Nor interest
To build with others
You offered me your soul
Handed it to me
A neatly packaged present
A brightly colored bow
No fear
No apprehension
A pureness that made me cry

I pressed my lips tightly together
Held my breath
For what I might disclose
I danced around you
Vague answers I used
To intellectualize
Bob and weave
Bob and weave
No strategy escaped you

...gasp...

Who are you?

Who are you to me?
Who are you who sees me as I am?
Offers me his beautiful soul
To cherish
Hold tightly
In trust
And love

You are one whose soul
Holds many doors
Some open
Some cracked
Some closed
None...locked
The accessibility you have offered
Unconditionally
Makes me say yes
And who could help it?
Your playful and innocent soul
Withstanding the worst
Of many tragedies

Still
You fight for your life
Infuse it with love
That which will help you
Replace externally sought resolution
External filling for the holes in your soul
With a blossoming internal healing
Grounded in the security of self-love

You will get there
Where you need to go
You whose touch
Embrace
Caress
Makes my body shiver
Whose lips I can still taste
Long after he leaves

Whose body intertwines with mine
Allowing me to disappear into a perfect bliss

I see you too
I see your struggle
Your fight
The pain that lives on the surface
Crawls across your skin
Begs you to find safety
In the arms of another

And I will be that other
As long as you will allow me
I will be the person who cheers for you
Celebrates
The vigor and vim you apply
To every aspect of your healing

With your transparency
Authenticity
Raw innocence
You have forced the pendulum
To the side of love and romance
No longer may I claim
Indifference

INTO THE FOLD

Wanting to bring you into the fold
It's true
The more you accept
With such gratitude
The more I choose to offer

My kindness
Is unlimited
Especially when celebrated
My gifts are authentic
Delivered from a place
Of warmth and respect

I am a giver
Truly
It makes me happy
To bring someone
I care for
So deeply
Into the fold
The circle
Where healthy, balanced, and reciprocal relationships
Exist
And expand
Graciously
For newcomers

INTUITION

My intuition tells me
Remove any unnecessary distractions
Be completely present
See this through
Wherever it leads

There's a way you look at me
You want me
You want me to want you
I do
I will
For how long?
How long will we be on fire
To what extent do we want this to build
Allowing ourselves to step closer and closer
Towards each other
Our souls connecting
In the throes of a passion
For which there are no words

I can imagine you
Someone to me
A priority
Wonder how you imagine me

I am indeed present
For you and this
Following an intuition that tells me
Trust
Step towards
Where I am sure to grow
Learn
Perhaps
Love

LEVEL

You meet me on a different level
Elevate my soul
To a space that is boundless
Where I am without context or reference
For how I feel
Where you take me
Took me
Have me

LEDGE

There we are
See us?
Standing all along the ledge
Some of us
Our faces to the sun
Drawn to
And fed by
Its warmth
Glorious rays

Some of us
Trying
Looking up
Down
Uncertain
Unstable
Un

Some of us
Fearing the unknown
The ledge
Sky above
Drop below
We are immobile
Inert

Some of us
Stand
Screaming
Scourge of pain
With the presentation
Of height
Depth

Some of us
Jump
An ending we welcome
In the blindness
Of
No
Other
Way

Some of us
Clasp hands
With those beside us
We know the powerful connection
The intricate weaving
Lace
Of our humanity
Prepares us
For any and all
Outcomes

LOVE

So down
So low
To question
Worth
Am I loveable?
Even when the circumstances
Of my life
Illuminate my flaws
Strategically guide me
Towards a path of self-destruction
Invite me to succumb
Encourage my focus
Away
From what I know I *can* be
My capabilities
Abilities
Unwavering determination
Will to survive

To love as I love
All that I am
And have
Given freely
Because somewhere along the way
Some
Albeit few
Have loved me
When the circumstances
Of my life illuminated my flaws
Strategically guided me
Towards a path of self-destruction

And I did indeed
Self-destruct
Over and
Over and
Over again

In my lifetime
I was introduced to
Maintained
An intimate relationship
With *every* dark
Frightening
Side of myself
Beasts best hidden from others
So, I ran
Still run sometimes
When I have/had to

Lying in a heap on the floor
Hiding in the shadows
Filled with so much pain
I saw no other recourse
But to pour it on others
Saturating them with my misery

Existing only by breath
Compromised
In every possible way
Warm hands reached out
Loving arms were extended
Pulling me towards clarity
Stability
Survival
Peace
Surrounded me
With love
And in valuing who I was
Infused and solidified
My sense of worth

I love as I have been loved
I love others in darkness
Through darkness to light

I share the best parts of myself
Knowing in feeding the soul of another
I feed my own

We are all connected
To each other
To the earth
With love as a conduit
We provide one another with strength
Pour joy into hearts
Where none exists
Hold hope for others
When it is noxious
Unfathomable
Gift it to others
In manageable doses
With patience
Kindness
And understanding

When I reflect on my life
I am overcome with gratitude
For having felt loved
By every person
Who saw beyond
The flaws of my humanity
Loved me
When I was covered in dirt
Soaked in a sludge I once thought
Defined me

I am even more grateful
For those who let me love them
As I love
With all that I am
And have
Those persons who allow
The reciprocity and balance of love
To nurture our relationship

Regardless of possession
Material wealth
Or the superficiality that gets in the way
Blocks the expression
Of pure
Unadulterated
Love

I have rarely encountered opportunities
To be exactly who I am
Flaws
Foibles
To find my way in the best way
I know how
And still have the unconditional love
Of someone
Truly in my corner

Moreover, identifying others
Who accept the love I offer
Exactly as I offer it
Has been challenging
At best

I want to tell you
I am ever so grateful
For your love and friendship
And because you have allowed me to love you
Unconditionally
With the utmost respect
And loyalty to our friendship
The bond we have shared
Through more challenges in life
We could ever count
Over all these years
This relationship has afforded me
With a safe space
To be exactly who I am

And I know too
After forty plus years of friendship
The longest relationship I will ever have
That none will ever compare

For that
For you
For us
I am humbled, grateful
And forever in your debt

For Lisa, a most beautiful flower, and my sister for life!

MEANT

And so, it meant
I would reach out randomly
Say I love you
Because you just never know

I would say exactly what I was thinking
All the aspects of your life
That you share with me
An updated status of all things
Important to you and therefore
Important to me

A day of reflection
I think of everyone I love so much
How fleeting life can be
How everything can change in an instant
So, it means
I will reach out randomly
Say I love you

NO MORE LONELY NIGHTS

Maybe you have two arms
Two legs
Walk about unassuming
Fitting in
Just enough
Is it?
Or are you just different enough
That you will spend most of your time
Life
Unattached
Alone?

I like your smile
Evidence of a flame
Within
Still burns brightly
With the hope
Of finding your match
I think you will

Won't we?
Won't we all
Walking about
Fitting in
Just enough
Find someone who celebrates
Who and what we are

And won't it be magic
When we finally fall in love
Look like the couples we admire
Walking about
Fitting in
So much more than enough
Indeed
No more lonely nights
For us!

THAT MAN

I want that man
I **WANT** that man
I want **THAT** man
I want that **MAN**

MYSTERY

I saw you fall
To your knees
...the time it took to stand
Maintain hope
Of loving again

And you tried
And you did
With a heart you held open
Enough
For another to enter

Damn you are beautiful
So much inside you
All of it visible
Accessible
When you look into my eyes

Trust...
Your ability to trust
Contingent on your capability
Of cultivating another's trust
In you

Stepping first
For you
Is not unlike a bridge
In which the planks may be unsecure
Wanting something so badly
Cautious and strategic
About how you will obtain it
You entice another
Lead
Guide
Ensure safety

Until they step close enough
That you may take a step
And offer your trust in them

The *swirl* of light and dark tones
The physical connection enhanced
By souls that blend and gel
With an indescribable ease

In the mystery of you
And this
Your tenderness
An innocence I want to know
In the saturation of wonder
Of the complexities
Simplicities and multiple paradoxes
I find I am falling
falling
falling
For this man
Whose depth draws me closer
To him with each interaction
Whose mysteries I want to solve
Every time he presses his lips
Against mine

And I will

THE CALM

And so
The storm shall pass
And you
Precious tiny
Will find the calm

Bumps
Bruises
Lacerated soul
Painful and protracted
Process of mending
And she does
And she will

Be in it
This storm
Hold tightly
Through each *crash*
To the bough
No wave shall destroy you
From no pouring
Drenching
Will you drown
I know this
As I know you

Gather your mighty strength
This day
For when the treachery of this storm passes
The sun will beam brightly through clouds
Opening to its powerful rays
And you...
You will set sail into your peace
Into the calm

THE MIRROR

Early on
Around the time when we first met
I sat across from you
Tears in my eyes
Someone had broken my fragile heart
Pained me
Made me question everything
I hold dear about who and what
I am
With your words
Kindness
Genuine care and concern
You healed my wound
Reminded me of all that I am
And have to offer

Years later
A horrific breakup
From which, I thought
I would never recover
Once again
You opened your heart to me
Reminded me I am worthy
And deserving
Of the love I desire

Just the other day
I landed on your doorstep
Soaked in a puddle of tears
We sat at your table
I was fully aware your time
Freedom from the responsibilities of your life
Held limits I might never understand
Yet
You listened
You held my broken, little heart in your hands
While I cried about the woes of my life

Many of which, are fleeting
Perhaps even insignificant
On the spectrum of those concerns
Which warrant a good cry

Still
You validated
Cared
Reinforced my strength
To move forward
Intact

I had a conversation with someone the other day
We talked about persons we value
Love
Aspire to emulate
In as many ways possible
And of course
You were the first person
Who came to mind

So, what is it about you?
What is it that I see...
Others see...
Something of which
You may not even be aware
Defines you
Your gift
The gift I see
Benefit from
And cherish in you...

You see into a person's soul
All that makes them beautiful
Worthy
Loveable
Extraordinary
Then
You reflect back what you see

Your soul a mirror
A critical illumination
Of truth
Clouded
Eclipsed by pain
And in this moment
A powerful, life-changing connection
Feeds the soul of another
Heals
That is your gift

It is for *all*
Not just those in your circle
For others have noticed it too
Yet I
As one so fortunate to be a part of your life
Have the opportunity to experience this
Each time you show up for me
When life slings a load of bricks
Across my path

Thank you!
Thank you for all the times you were there
Not just with a smile
Cup of hot coffee
Glass of Pinot Grigio
Comforting hug
The safety of a hand to hold
Thank you for sharing the gift
Of the mirror in your soul
Especially with me
And know that it has saved me
Rescued my heart
More times than I could ever count
Thank you too
For making a difference in my life
Every single day you are in it

For my soul sister Jen, a most beautiful flower indeed!

THE UNIVERSE SHIFTED

The universe shifted when...

I found I connected more with the old than the young

I no longer punished myself for both careless and sophisticated
mistakes

Despite my dissatisfaction with my physical appearance, the visibility
of my aging process, physical changes which initially devasted me, I
came to celebrate I am more than the vessel that contains my soul

I was certain the choices I made with all things, I made from the
best space in which I could make them

In the process of gaining true self-acceptance, I learned the value of
accepting others

I learned to trust my instincts and walk away from toxicity

Loving myself was no longer something to strive for...indeed I did
and do, and loving myself became my protection

WHAT IF

You scare the hell out of me...

Snapping my little fingers
I danced around my kitchen
Looked to you
Your eyes closed
Arms swinging to the music
No longer
"Too chicken to dance"

Who are you
Where did you come from?
Cliché
And no less real

I was intrigued by the parallels
In our values
The importance we place on connection
The organic evolution of what develops
A foundation of friendship
Freedom to be who we are
Choose to share a space
Or not

I could see it
The possibility of you
With me
A friendship filled with conversation
Music
Concerts
Laughter
Sharing
Nights of dancing
In my kitchen
Snapping our fingers
And miles and miles of
What if

WHENEVER YOU GO

When you left
I dove into my bed
Could smell your body
Smell *us*
All over the room

I'm falling for you
Just as I spin when you make love to me
Touch me in ways
I haven't been touched in decades
Maybe forever

I don't know what you do to me
When my body quivers
My heart pounds
My soul satiated
I don't know how I will keep getting into this bed
Without you in it
When I want you so badly
Crave your skin against mine
A connection that leaves me breathless

You are beautiful
Radiate light
Goodness
Kindness
Leave me with the warmth of your spirit
The scent of you
And a fulfilment I have not known
For way too long

...Whenever you go

WORTH THE TIME

Patient
Through my perpetual underestimation
Of time and task
No lecture
Nor roll of the eyes
Simply
True understanding

I asked a question
Planned to avoid answering
You responded succinctly
Directed it towards me
Rather than punt
I circumvented
An existential and philosophical tangent
From which your innocent sarcasm
Caused me to return

Touched me
The way I love to touch another
Took my breath away
In the darkness of your sanctuary
Where your heart and soul were open
For my exploration

You step towards me without misstep
That which I am sure will occur
And never does
Your invitations
Most welcomed
Leave me stunned
Confused
Desperate to hide

You're correct
I **am** scared
It just feels much too easy
What lies around the corner?
Hovers in the shadows
Narcissism
Arrogance
Deceitfulness

Does the caution I exercise
Maintain distance between us
My safety and self-protection
Weighing down a progression
An opportunity for me
To move forward with you
To remain synchronized with you
To find that I could
Without question
Fall
Fall
Fall
For you

Your accessibility is absolutely, lovely
The clarity in the presentation of your wants
Needs
The self-directed navigation
Of all spaces you occupy
A confidence that intrigues and excites me
A boldness that like a magnet
I gravitated towards from the moment we met

You scare the hell out of me
And I won't tell you that
Yet
You will know
Do know
The question is
Is it enough for you

I will need time
Find my own footing
Fearless that I am
Albeit never in love

If only I could spread my arms
Run into the breeze
Wind
Storm
Or ruin
Just give me the time
I am worth the time
Worth the time

OVER A DECADE

It occurred to me
I haven't fallen in love with someone
In over a decade

I have fallen for people
Believing
Eventually I'd fall in love
Until I didn't

To truly fall in love
Like I did when we met
Feel and watch myself slipping
Accept the inevitability
Of a love that washed over me
Warm like North Carolina summer rain
A locomotive
That flattened me
In the best sort of way

No
I have not fallen in love
Madly
Hopelessly
Desperately
In over a decade

I hope to love again
Yet
If I do not
I am grateful to have known
The allure
Breathlessness
Timelessness
Of heart stopping love
Once seen in the eyes
Of one who loved me

CALL

I thought I'd call you this morning
While I swigged coffee
Ate my toast
I missed you
Missed hearing your voice

I wanted to call you
Every time I met someone
Got a job offer
Had a great date
Needed to make a decision

I wanted to tell you
How I was feeling
Hear about you
Your day
Laugh out loud

It's going to be OK
When I have to live my life
In the absence of something
That meant everything to me

It's going to be OK
Not because it's easy
And the pain isn't palpable
But because I did have that call
I had a long string of calls
That reinforced our love for each other
And even though I can't call you now
You gave me enough conversations
Based in joy and love
To last forever

SAD HEART

Sad, tired heart
Protect it
Nurture it
Until it is strong enough
To love again

MY LOVE

This is what my love looks like
Vinicunca, rainbow mountains of Peru
Blue waters of the Maldives
A view that takes your breath away

This is what my love tastes like
Belgian chocolate
Salted caramel
So sweet you'll let it sit on your tongue

This is what my love sounds like
Beethoven's Moonlight Sonata
Nina Simone's Wild is the Wind
Music you can hear with your soul

This is what my love feels like
A cotton blanket fresh from the dryer
Sun exposed linen taken from a clothesline
Soft protection to wrap all around you

This is what my love smells like
Homemade bread from the oven
The morning after a fresh rain
Enveloping

This is who you are when I love you
A timeless treasure I value
Every day
The person with whom I grow old
Whose scrunched up
Wrinkly little face
Tells stories
Narrated by
A voice that opens my heart

This is who I am when I love you
One who sits wrapped in a blanket
Beside you
Listening and lost in your stories
Yours
And forever celebrating
How completely in love with you
I am

Wildflowers...

CRY

I'm going to cry
Fill the room with tears
That will carry me away
I will trust it
Because I know it flows to a waterfall
That will hurl me down
I will crash
Gasp for air
Beg for my life
I will survive
Flow along the river
And it will be tranquil
Again

JUDGE

There's a tub of butter in my bed
A box of crackers
A tub...
Sounds bigger than it is
Never mind
Just don't judge me
It sounds worse than it is
It's a snack
While I rest on cotton sheets
And soft blankets

Were it a glass of vodka
Neat
What then?
It has been
In the past
Although sometimes rocks

Or was it jug of cheap wine?

Judge if you must
It's not what it seems

Still judging?
Stop what you're doing
Right now
What's in your bed?

SUMMER SEX

Summer sex
You say
The kind of sweaty
Summer sex
Where human physical imperfections
Are completely ignored
In favor of enhancing
A liberating
Raw
Unparalleled tryst

He has a look about him
Sees through me
Allows me to peer through a keyhole
Enough to affirm
It feels like more

Is it?
Or is it a one-sided
Love affair
Perceived complete package
The inevitable hurt
Of unrequited love
Around the corner

Don't care
It's a hot
Sticky
Steamy summer
And with it
A slippery exploration
The enveloping pleasures
Of sweaty
Summer sex

GOING SOMEWHERE

I'm going somewhere
Right now
Headed out
See ya

I'm going to say
Good bye
Like I have
Like we do
Miss you
Like a lost girl
Even though
All aspects of my life
Demonstrate the most precise aim

I want to go somewhere
With one who understands
Values my complexities
Cherishes me
Imperfections
Peculiarities
Rusty parts
Makeshift repairs
And all

I want to head out
Take off
With you
On a journey
Laugh until we cry
A team
Unstoppable
Unbreakable
In each other's arms
Hearts
Souls

Still
I search
I know you're out there
Looking for me

In the interim
I'm floating about
Loving myself
My adventure

A butterfly
Going somewhere
Right now
Headed out
See ya!

HAPPY BIRTHDAY IRMA

So, I'm thinking about
The times of your life
Which have intersected with mine
The ways we connected
Disconnected
And strategies we used to rebuild
During periods of weak scaffolding

People often ask
Do you long for someone with whom you can grow old?
Aging is inevitable
I am advancing in years
Embracing every phase of my life with acceptance
Because of the gift
Of being surrounded
By those who love me
And allow me to love them
I have *more* than a someone
I, like you
Have many

It has been nearly two decades since we began this journey
Of friendship
Sisterhood
We have leaned on each other through loss
Coached each other
Through the navigation
Of the most challenging obstacle courses
Shared in the triumphs and fears
Of motherhood
Told each other stories
That brought the years when we didn't know each other
To life

It is your birthday
A day that marks
Half a century

A life well-lived
A tale told of perseverance
And unwavering fortitude
Even when you wondered from where
You would draw strength
To get through a day
Hour
Or simply
To breathe

In this moment
You are surrounded by everyone
Who chooses to grow old with you
Their faces smiling
Eyes filled with the authentic love
That has raised and held you
All of your life
And I
While absent physically
Have sent my love
Support
Friendship and sisterhood
A presence
In spirit

We are all here
We love you
And wish for you
Transition into your next half century
With joy
Excitement
Thrills
And a peaceful end to each day
Where you may reflect on your purpose
And feel the warmth you have brought to all of us

For Irma, a sister whose strength is unwavering!

NEW YEAR'S EVE

No one should spend New Year's Eve alone
Unless it's their choice
And that choice is made
While content in their own company
In peace
With sincere gratitude
An abundance of love in their heart
For self and others

A cup of something warm
Pondering
Recalling success
Choices made with clarity
Ignorance
Acceptance of outcomes
Of the passing year
Possibilities of the next

Happiness is not contingent
On the presence of others
On this day
Or any
Happiness is a garden
We spend a lifetime nurturing
Even when the weeds are thriving
And considerable time is spent
Pulling them
We do
With the force we need
To ensure they do not return
And should they
We are prepared to pull again

We grow what we love
Abolish what we do not
Year after year

And should we take the last day
To reflect on our work
Alone
We do this in love
Kindness to ourselves
Celebration of who we are
Who we may become
In the presence of a new year

OTHER SIDE OF THE CALL

Eager to discover
What's on the other side
Of every call
Moments you made me laugh
Your words
Strung together
Guide me
Towards a growing desire for you

I am drawn in easily, effectively
By the sound of your voice
Curious about the intensity
Of your command
The electrical charge
On the other side
Of the call

Images you create
Strategically infuse
Saturate my mind
Cause my body to respond
To a touch
I can easily imagine
Convinces me
In reality
I will be left breathless

The sound of your voice
Arouses me
I crawl through the phone
Must reach you
Have you

So, you'll stun me with your direct
And ever so welcomed
Encouraged
Erotic dialogue
Words I paint along the lines of my body
While we tell stories
That eventually
Will bring us an ease
We can sink into
When finally
We meet

PERSONAL

It was all personal
Every last bit of it
Not just clients or patients
Humans
Whose lives I changed
Who changed mine

My mother lie dying
I kissed her cheek
Told her I loved her
Went back to work
Her unconscious state
My saving grace

It's personal
Every effort
Every dime of my own money
No overtime
In the face of furlough
A relentless productivity wheel
That turned clients into widgets
On a never-ending conveyor belt
The shame of knowing
I didn't
Couldn't
Give them my very best

All that I gave
Give
Pieces of my soul
In exchange for a most incredible connection
The beauty in being present
Through the growth of another
Their presence for mine

It's personal!

And how absolutely sad
Disheartening
When that element of shimmering gold
We selflessly offer others
If not undervalued
Falls completely lost on management

You're damn right it's personal!
This *is* my life
And theirs

I'm not a cashier
Checking out a customer
I'm using my gifts
To help people
Reach and teach them
Fully present with others
In their darkest hours
Watching them thrive
In brightness
And love

Simply knowing I was a small part of that
Is just powerful enough
To make it personal

SAVED FROM SUICIDE

You saved me from *SUICIDE* when you

S – Thanked me for the birthday card
U – Said I was a good mother
I – Told me you liked my laugh
C – Said I was not alone
I – Said I was a good friend
D – Called and invited me to lunch
E – Complimented my outfit

Told me I was loved

S – Reminded me of my purpose
U – Walked up to me and wagged your tail
I – Offered to buy me breakfast
C – Rode coasters with me
I – Watched a movie with me
D – Held my hand when we went hiking
E – Toddled up to me and let me hold you on my lap

Showed me I was loved

S – Licked my face with your dog breath
U – Brought me flowers just because
I – Offered to bring me food when I was sick
C – Sat with me when I cried
I – Sang songs with me
D – Held me tightly
E – Made love to me and took my breath away

Loved me

S – Convinced me there is someone for everyone
U – Brushed my hair
I – Washed my clothes
C – Fixed my car
I – Hired me
D – Showed up on the worst day of my life
E – Danced with me

Told me I was loved
Showed me I was loved
Loved me

SECRET

One month to the day

Tell me

Falling, falling, falling

Tell me

Rushed towards each other
Blinding momentum
Breathless

Tell me

The weight of you
Warmth of your body
Scent of your skin

Tell me

Taste of your lips

Tell me

Yes, and now
To all

Tell me

Don't want to imagine
Touching
Being touched by another
Since you

Tell me

Your voice when you sing
Speak

Tell me

Softly trace
The lines of my body

Tell me

Our souls communicate
We are synchronized

Tell me

I know already
I've known
I need you to say it
Disclose the truth

Tell me

Tell me

Tell me

Your **secret**

TAPE

I knew he wasn't "the one"
My person
When we did not connect
In a space of mutual grounding
Stability

I see him
He embraces healing
With such grace
Dignity
Gratitude and knowing
It makes me cry to witness
Yet
This is only the beginning
Of his journey
And I the reinforcement
To his self-affirmation
Another among many
Rolls of tape
He rightfully
Deservedly
Collects
Along his path to the wholeness
His soul seeks
And undoubtedly
Will find

How did I know?
It was in the expression
Of his desire
For what he needs
The telling
Retelling
Of all that makes him beautiful
Because he has not yet realized
He is already seen

Humans shatter like glass
Sharp pieces and shards
Defenses against the likelihood
Probability
Of more breaks and cracks
With every move

Slowly
He picks up the pieces
His crushed
Damaged soul
Each tender word spoken by another
Unconditional deed
The strength he uses
To mend

So, I did
I realized his fragility
The potential for words
Spoken in play
To propel him back
To a place of pain
Stepping towards him
Slowly
A necessary tiptoe
Just to be allowed in

His kiss
A different kind of longing
Than mine
The expression of his need
For more tape
I complied
Wrapped my love around him
Each caress
Affirmation
Bringing him closer

Creating a space of love
Kindness
Safety

Yet the imbalance of our needs
In this moment
Confirm for me
I am a healer for him
And he is much too fragile
To meet me
Where I stand
To add to my collection
Of strong houses
With old bones
Solid
As I

Over many hours
We danced
Kissed
Made love
Exchanged tales
Of blood and gore
Peace and joy
The resulting serenity
Only achieved
When one rises from the bludgeoning
In life
We are certain
We will never survive

In the light of day
After swirling in the drift
Of candlelight
I found time for reflection
You will fall in love with this man
The visibility and experience
Of knowing a soul

That moves through tragedy with such
Determination
One who recognizes opportunities
For healing
Seeks them out
Leans in with courage
Conviction
Yes
You could fall for him
Will
And sadly
The distance between where you are
On your journey
Where he is
On his
So great that you will mistakenly choose
To suspend your own growth
Continued movement towards what is integral
To your own progression

He is not where you are
And you cannot stop
Or step backwards to meet him
Simply because of the magnetism
And illuminating coloration
Of his precious and innocent
Soul

So, I will meet you
In the crossing
Hold you in my arms
Love you with all my heart
Add more tape
Support you in your journey
Towards healing
Wholeness on which
Your life depends

Until your worth is so well grounded
It no longer needs
External affirmation

Then I will keep walking
For I know the one
Whose distance achieved
On the journey
Progress
Demonstrated evidence of solid grounding
In every way
Aligns with my own
Has yet to be found

WHAT MATTERS

I reconcile and accept
Because that's what I do
And the moment I want an Italian Beef sandwich
I remember what it's going to take to date someone
Who runs marathons
And it sure isn't an Italian Beef body
So rather than ruling you out
Before you rule me out
I will present everything about me that is important and meaningful
Which is, no matter what evidence exists of my food choices
I am fit and healthy
Even more important
My health is multi-dimensional
I am emotionally, physically, spiritually, and soulfully healthy

Why does that matter?
Should we choose each other?
Your morning run
My desire to sleep in
Your light snack
My big bowl of pasta
My 30 minutes on an elliptical
Your triathlon
None of these matter
If we have fallen wildly in love
Have mind-blowing sex
And are determined to add only sheer joy, love, and laughter
To each other's lives
The outside not nearly as important
As the inside

Here's an idea
Don't judge me
I won't judge you
Instead
Let's focus only on
What matters

WATCHER

Maybe you'll see
As I sit on the side
In the crowd
Yet not *of* it
I am not the one for you
Or perhaps anyone
Am I?

I say
I'm not a joiner
I'm not
I wonder about your ability
To let me be
Who
What
I am
A writer
Watcher
Voyeur
Who chooses carefully selected
Experiences
Like the most unique
Wildflower
Among many
In a vast field

While you may believe me apathetic
In my non-participatory status
I am a watcher
Voyeur
Who simply
Joins in other ways

Should you therefore imagine my choice
To sit on the sidelines
As a lack of interest
You will be mistaken
You will have missed
Who I am
A soul who observes
Absorbs
Immerses
In my own
Very special way

THE WAY I SHOULD HAVE

I didn't do anything
The way I should have

I should have
Cultivated more family relationships
Used precision and foresight
To hand-pick
A person with whom
I would bring another soul into this world
Worked harder
Studied more
Partied *wwwaayyy* less
Loved with more discretion
Chose battles with more discernment

I tried
I tried with zeal
Dug for it
Some semblance of self-love and respect
Just enough
For just enough
And survived

I'm intact
You see that
Don't you?
I sit alone in many rooms
Albeit enchanting spaces
Adorned in tapestry
Sip tea
Reflect
With gratitude
On the magic that was/is
My life

Still
I have yet to find my place
In this world
Reluctant
Opposed
To prioritizing
Comfort
Over adventure

For I crave
A most delicious journey
My travels telling me
Exactly what I need to know
About the balance
Between how I should have navigated
A life with so many roads
And the celebration
Of those choices well made

THE RISK

What of the risk?
Your lips so close to mine
I feel your breath upon them
It takes everything I have
Not to kiss you

Blah and boring
This sport
That fishing
Excerpts and authors
More than I ever wanted to know
About wine
Please!
Just drink the damn glass!

Dating
Waiting
Wish it was you
Wish you saw through my distance
Casual banter
The times I pretended we were buddies

Your uniquely good looks
Caricature face
Toothy smile
Your pensive expression
Shifting the instant
I have said something to which
You connect

I love your stories
Resourceful and resilient
Lineage
I see you are much like
The parents you describe

Damn you're pretty
In the red light
Of a room I have staged
For your visit
I could talk to you for hours
Make love to you
The same

What of the risk?
That I should step up and say
I'd like to pick you!
The dating a needless backdrop
To this connection we have

What of the risk?
That I should say
You may not fit my exact criteria
But damn!
You are somethin!

What of the risk?
That I wish would take the place
Of
Safe

REPLICATION

It might have taken me
Forever
Finally
I got it

I realized
So many of my relationships
Were replicated by those
Of my past
The toxic ones
The dirty toilet bowl
In a roadside gas station ones
The ones I fought to escape
Ran from
Like I was on fire
And then
I replicated them
Duplicated them

Perplexed by repeated suffering
Scratched my little head
Forced myself to see
Take off the glasses
Of illusion

And when I finally
Saw myself
Chasing my tail
In a cycle
When finally
I recognized the dirt
Dust
Smeared soil
Darkening my life
I made a change

Cutting off
Moving on
Slamming the door
Letting go
Asking for
Deserving more

I left you
And the mirror images of you
She
He
They
Same person
Different faces

In recognizing this
I grew
Exponentially
No longer doomed to replicate

UNDER THE RUBBLE

You
Me
And all your past lovers
Those who molded
Shaped you
Into who you are
The contributions
You took and take on
As you continue to evolve

We will all spend time together
All of us
Get to know each other
Throughout the course
Of the complicated task
Of peeling away their negativity
Down to the core identities
Where we will surely and finally
Match

That is what we are...
An amalgam of all we have absorbed
Integrated
Struggling to know our true selves
Just well enough to share that truth
With others
Hoping to find a genuine and lasting match
Click
With what is under
The rubble